sad but not depressed

sad love poetry collection

ali ashraf

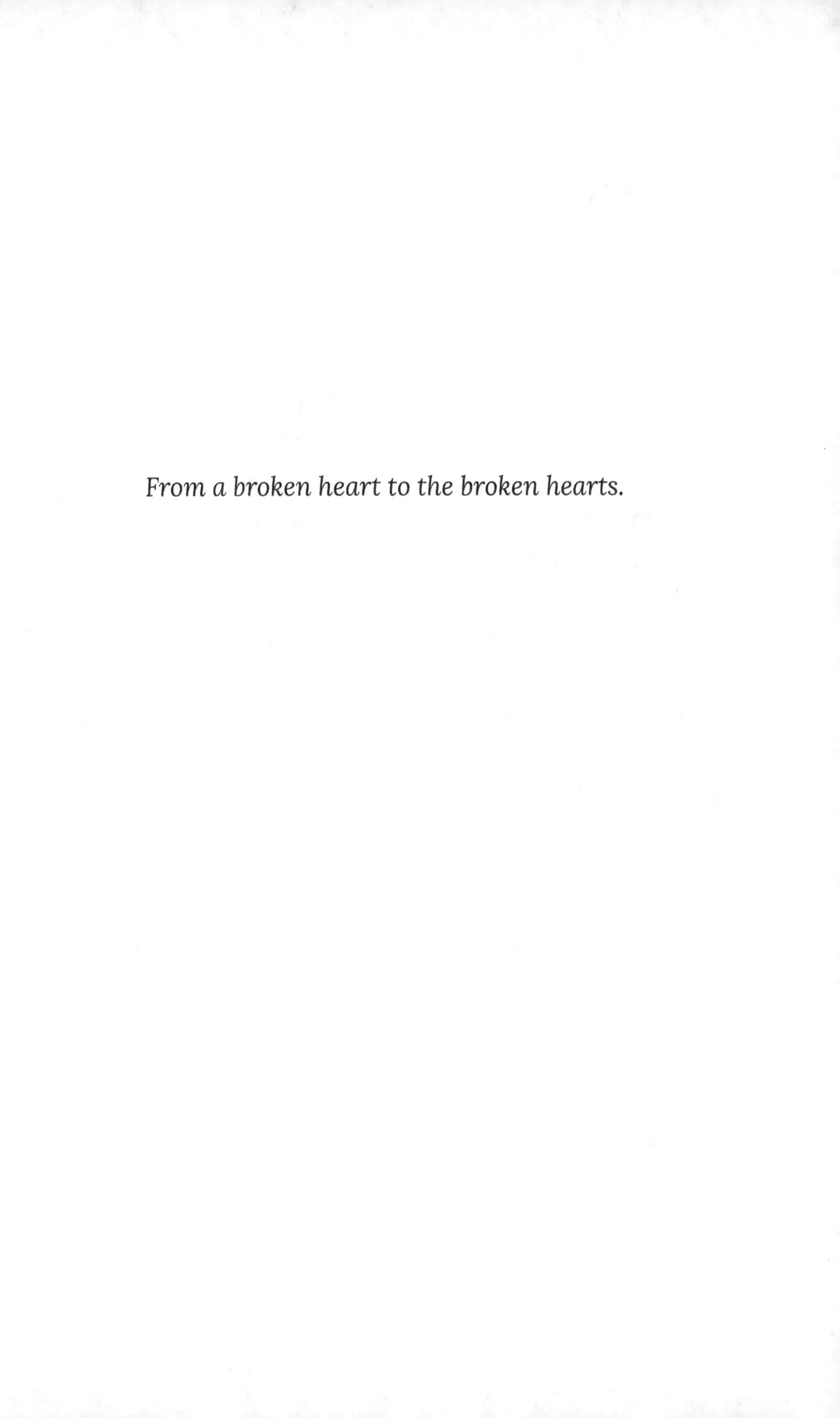

From a broken heart to the broken hearts.

Preface

Let's leave this cold depressing place and go somewhere where we can be sad together, where the sweet melancholy reminds us of the good old days. Depression is overbearing and unpredictable. It makes us feel unwanted and makes our hearts heavy without a reason. We gnaw at our existence and feel a desire for self-hurt and self-destruction. Hands down I'd always choose sadness over depression because sadness heals over time, it has elements of hope and patience somewhere deep down in its existence. A hope that things will be better someday. A hope that patience will change the course of our lives over time. Whereas depression has elements of anxiety and suicidal tendencies at worst.

This book attempts to touch upon both depression and sadness and tries to transform the depression into sadness

So let's find a place to be sad rather than depressed. Let's find solace in patience and melancholy. Let's beat depression with sadness. I am not an expert on depression but that's how I believe we can cope with it.

-   Ali Ashraf (Suhrawardi)

POEMS

POEMS

These Days

you left me amid the storm
cruelty has become a norm
these days

you left me amid the storm
I am feeling so alone
these days

I see you wherever I go
you are here since you've gone
these days

I know you never loved me
but I can't move on
these days

love was my mistake
you are not to blame
I am reaping the fruits
of what I had sown
these days.

Last Memory

there's a flickering flame
within my heart
that starts and stops
comes and goes
like a ray of hope
    yes, it's bright
    no, it's not

what should I do with it?
fuel it or let it die
my ray of hope
my only chance
my tears drop
    yes, it's bright
    no, it's not

within my sighs
along my cries
it was so bright
all the time
now starting to stop
    yes, it's bright
    no, it's not

it's my only recollection
of time gone by
it's my last memory
this flickering light
and there it goes
        not bright anymore
        now it's not.

Forget All That

forget all that
what you heard
what she said
forget all that

it was all a dream
that broke all your dreams
don't be sad
forget all that

she came like spring
like autumn she went
it was all a phase
forget all that

the moon is still here
the stars; they still shine
but wherever I see,
her face I don't find

what should I do?
what should I say?
without her
life is empty.

I still remember
all the promises she made
under the moonlight
forget all that

she came into my life
like a beautiful surprise
it was all a play
it was all a game

her love was a lie
her sweetness was a fraud
first, she brought joy
then only sadness she brought

the garden still lives
the trees still stand
but she is not here
forget all that

the flowers bloom
as the lovers meet
but if she is not here
nothing seems to be

how my heart she had
how she drove me mad
don't think about it now
forget all that.

Forget Her

let the music play a lovely tune
let the melody flow
like wine through my blood
so I can forget her

let me dance in a frenzy
until my whole body becomes numb
let me enjoy these festivities
so I can forget her

let me do flamenco
although I don't know how to
let me laugh until my stomach aches
so I can forget her

let me travel the entire world
exotic lands and meet different people
observe different cultures and traditions
so I can forget her

let me live and be free
from this love's cage
let me learn how it feels
to be living again
oh I waited so long to forget her

but wherever I go, what is this that I see?
an emptiness within me
she is like scars all over my body
why can't I seem to forget her?

My Words Are For You

my words are for you
I hope you remember me
as I remember you

your smile, your laughter
your words surround me
you are all around me

today it rained in my city
and I have no one to tell this
and I wept silently

my friends ask me about you
what should I tell them?
you disappeared without a clue

my words are for you
I hope someday you'll read them
and remember us, as I do

my words are for you.

Forgetfulness

I often forget the things
that I have to do
cause all I can remember
is loving you.

Oceans Apart

somewhere lost in books
the fragrance of love
somewhere lost in the fog
our breaths and cigarettes smoke
where have gone the carefree days?
O friend, time flew at a pace
yes, now we are oceans apart
but you always beat in my heart.

I Seek Love

I seek love in strange places
in forlorn deserts, in sad faces
I seek love in piercing glance
in waterfalls, in green fields
where fairies dance.

Daydreaming

raindrops, teardrops
misty winters of western lands
countryside, you by my side
your hand in my hand

raindrops, we smile
pitter-patter heard for a while
we find solace under a hut
kiss each other with our bold eyes

countryside, European lands
rain falls at our command
I miss our kiss, cut in half
I miss the future we'll never have.

Life

the day we're born
it seems to be
a new day, a new morn
a new dream

then childhood comes
of wanton gleams
and frightful fears
and cozy sleep

and then the youth
of another bloom
of hopes and wishes
of romance and doom

and then the adulthood
and then the old age
day passes into night
life disappears into haze.

The Eyes

the eyes that took me by surprise
I still miss those eyes

the eyes that were the comfort of my eyes
I still miss those eyes

the eyes that knew the sacrifice
I still miss those eyes

the eyes that knew all my cries
I still miss those eyes

the eyes that lit up my life
I still miss those eyes

the eyes that are nowhere to be seen
the eyes that saw my dreams with me
the eyes that disappeared from my sight
I still miss those eyes.

Love is Blind

love is blind, love is deaf
love came; now nothing's left
my life has become a stranded island
love is to blame for this theft

love is blind, love is deaf
it's a lie, I tell you
love is clever; it's a con
love will rob you like a fool

love is blind, love is deaf
love is a tyrant. love is cruel
yet it's the best feeling to have
by hook or crook, love's bound to rule.

My Heart Died With You

my heart died with you

my eyes beseech our union
that'll never be

my ears long for your whispers
like a lost dream

since you have left
I can't seem to breath

I can't seem to move
my heart died with you

did you forget the days when I cried with you?
my heart died with you.

One Glance

I have nothing left
you took everything with you
my smile, my mirth
even my tears dried up
how could you do this?

you took away all my emotions
all things that made me happy
now I don't like anyone,
I don't like anything
it feels as if I am dying.

you took away my laughter
my sweetheart, how sweet you are
and when you smile
my whole world lights up
why did you leave me?

I can't forget you
I just want to embrace you
and never let go
why? why did you do this?
why made my life so empty?

just one more gaze at your face
will bring back my breath
and I'll feel alive again
just one glance, one last chance
will put end to my misery
and I'll become sane.

Longing

alas there is no one near
yet I feel the presence appear
maybe its presence of shattered dreams
or the echo of my silent screams
people ask me why my face is so grim
because I hold severe pain within
and the darkness has overshadowed my life
it's been so long since I've seen the light
why is life so cruel to me?
unanswered questions lay surrounding
nowhere can I find a hope
nowhere for my soul to elope
no tears appear on my face
still, I cry and look for grace
and here I am sitting alone
lost in memories of days long gone
never will I see the day again?
it's been centuries since the sun last shone
it seems the time has come to freeze
cause in longing time ceases to exist
rose has withered and the nightingale cries
the garden filled with blood weeps and sighs
the flute only plays sad tunes
each flower has now started to die
where am I? what is this station?

where nothing exists but only patience
the clouds are crying in separation
the earth has started to seem barren
so many people came but left in the end
my heart is just a deserted land
waiting for so long that now I think
the only thing left in me is longing.

Indifference

how the things are
let them be
they tell me so ardently

but how could I turn away
my face and refuse
and accept the fact
that I am of no use.

The Window

I crave your intimacy
in cold winter nights
as the snow starts to creep in
through the open doors
and day after day
monotony prevails
I try to pinpoint my feelings
through barren words
and cool winter breeze
lurks in
I think I left the window open
I see a dervish dancing
as he shivers from cold
or maybe he is too old
or maybe I am too young
to comprehend
that nothing makes sense.

Limbo

all tears have dried
maybe I've moved on
or maybe I have died.

I Died

even in death
I dream of hugging you
don't love me now
I died loving you.

Winter Fog

long empty roads
cold winter fogs
life brought me here
tears and despair
never-ending nights
shivers and frights.

Graves

there are many graves
in my heart
but yours is the most
beautiful of them all.

Stains

although I've burned
all of your pictures
but how could I burn
what's imprinted on my heart?
even though it's burning.

although I've forgotten
what you said
but how could I forget
and peel off my skin?
that has your memory
like blood stains
living all over it
bleeding from time to time.

how could I undo
what's already done?
how could I walk
with broken bones?
that call your name
with each crack
and I know that I can't
live with you anymore
but how could I live
with this traitor

that beats inside me
still calls out your name.
how do I live with myself anymore?

Get Burned

my heart is a grave
where dead you lay
and get burned every day
by the ache in my heart
lay dead, my love
get burned, my love.

Under One Roof

under one roof
were the dreams,
was the beginning
when love was in bloom
under one roof

we loved and lived,
we touched and kissed,
we laughed with the kids
under one roof

but then we strayed
from the dreams we saw
from the boundaries we laid
under one roof

but we try to compromise
even when love dies
and the worse times arrive
under one roof

and I may have wronged
but I still long
to have a strong bond
under one roof

so please for our love's sake
the future is at stake
let us happily stay
under one roof.

Dear Future Wife

dear future wife,
have you lost your mind?
cause if you have lost it
I have lost it too.

in that case
there is no trouble
don't you worry
we'll make a great couple

but if you are sane
and still want to be mine
then my love
you're losing your mind.

Without You, I am Helpless

without you, I am helpless
I am floating away like hay
I feel cold and shiver in the summer
in winter, I feel breathless

without you, I am helpless
my eyes scream of your unfaithfulness
my heart pounds in my chest
it tells horrors that I have seen
it tells about your ruthlessness
without you, I am helpless

my soul is stained with your memories
the winter breeze brings your fragrance
I wake up in my bed alone
by my side, only your remembrance
without you, I am helpless

I am breathing and killing my days
I know someday I'll move on too
but right now I feel suffocated
with million rocks on my chest
without you, I am helpless.

In Separation

in separation
all hope disappears
those who smile in separation
will smile forever.

Belongings

the tears you gave me
are my only belongings
I have lost everything else.

Echoes

your voice echoes
through my dark days
your memories,
they keep me going.

Only If You Were Here

if you were here
I would've held you tight
and all the sorrows that I hide
would disappear
only if you were here

if you were here
we would've danced together
laughed and giggled
without any fear
only if you were here

if you were here
I would've felt alive again
I never could've died again
a new hope would've appeared
only if you were here

but you are not here
and I am all alone
I sing sad songs
think of the time that's gone
I think my death is near
and you are not here.

We Are Never Really Apart

life goes on
and mine does too
but not too alone
along with memories of you

I travel the world
I travel to different lands
when I see something exciting
I imagine what you would've said

when I eat some exotic food
of some exotic land
I see your hand in my hand
I see you passing comments

you are always with me
in my mind and my heart
I am never too alone
we are never really apart.

My Prayers Are With You

my sweet love
my prayers are with you
may happiness ever surrounds you
may all your worries disappear
may your life never have
a single sorrowful tear.

Spark of Love

spark of love
would it ever go away?
it keeps on coming back
and turns into a flame

I've been in love many times
my heart broke again and again
now I am afraid of falling in love
I don't want to fuel this flame

I am falling into despair
I only have myself to blame
I can't fuel this flame, I am scared
I won't fall in love again.

November Rain

as we went down
the memory lane
November rain
brought pain.

January

every January brings a new year
I wish it also brought a new me
I wish it also brought you along
I wish we could finally live free.

April

all months come and go
so does the month of April
but our grim faces often show
we're sad, our hearts aren't well.

May

we said what we had to say
in the month of may
but this longing doesn't end at all
it is here to forever stay.

July

in July
you kissed my eye
we learned to fly
in July
you cut my wings
you made me cry
now I could never fly
in July.

August

so august went too
like all the months do
and you never came
my life remains the same.

September

Oh, I still remember
your smile in September
when the sun shone on us
your hair looked so amber

I still remember
our love in September
my kisses made you giggle
on your body slender

Oh, I still remember
our meetings of September
it all seems a dream now
I've woken up from slumber.

October

I was not sober
all this October
I was sad and drunk
in your eyes sunk.

November

rains and fogs November brings
my heart suppresses a tumult within
all year passed in reflective gazes
life alone; combined with puzzling mazes
lovers alone and aloof do stand
I see sand escaping my hand.

Happy Holidays

snowflakes
frozen lakes
misty breaths
eyes blurry wet
children giggle far away
the season of lovers has come neigh
leaves wither and die
lovers mourn and sigh
neighbours come and pry
"any plans for New Year's?"

"I will cry alone
on these winter nights"
I reply

Everlasting Misery

the everlasting misery
has made a home in my veins
my thoughts insane
I vomit sighs
and bleed your longing
from my eyes.

Shallow

my poetry makes them cry
who thought
my tears weren't real.

Dark Love

the seducing and entrapping
mistress of death
who lives somewhere
in a faraway land

has had me in her spell
with her bewitching tricks
she has stolen my heart
and in its search
I wander the streets and bazaar

this is not love
this is something dark
this is something sinister
I feel myself falling into hell's pit
being lulled by the devil's minister

who would save my soul now?
I see dead people
wherever I go, I see black crows
and owls hanging upside down
God, help me now.

Lullaby

after a long tiring day
the night comes
and silence surrounds the world
lovers are long asleep
in each other's arms

nothing is said
nothing can be heard
the world is lulled into
a silence so deep
at that moment I am awake
and your memories wake up with me.

Castle of Sand

remember our promises
of eternal love?
of "I'll always love you"
of happily ever after?

was my hand not enough to hold?
what made you hold someone else's hand?
our love was thin air
our promises; a castle of sand
when the waves of time hit
we saw our inevitable end

now all of that seems
like a childhood dream
lost in our foggy memories
haunting back in our sleep
a part of our suppressed egos
a part of our unconscious stream

that's why without a reason we cry
that's why we often feel down
and we never seem to know why
but deep down we know why
and deep down we know how

we realized at an age so young
that if you and I can grow apart
then in this changing world
nothing can forever last

that's why we cry without a reason
but let's name it maturity
and change the perception
and pose this forever lost love
as a great achievement.

Depressed

I miss the time
when the light of love
entered my soul
now I am filled
with hate and remorse
I feel so cold
I am so numb and dead
I'd better die instead
than faking life
my miserable waking life
I want to fall asleep.

Stuck

right-wing, left-wing
genome editing
technology and doom
political boom
everywhere there's noise
everywhere crowds
but where's love?
where's the human touch?
where's the feeling that allows
us to be content

the world is changing so fast
and here I am
almost out of breath
with my hand on my heart
and your memories deep inside
not being able to move on.

Suffocation

I see you and my heart beats so fast
I feel I am going out of breath
I feel so angry at myself
this is not love, it's suffocation
I want to hate you but admiration
jumps in, and I feel so confused
thoughts in my mind bang drums huge
I feel like I am losing my temper
I want to hurt you but I remember
our love that once was and I sigh
and burst into tears and start to cry.

Walking Dead

like the worms eat
a rotting corpse
your love ate
life out of my soul
I am walking dead
and tears I shed
are of blood
sucked out of my veins
my life in vain
my existence in pain
I gnaw myself
to feel alive
I feed myself to beasts
to know if I am living
but whatever I do
adds to my fall
I don't feel
anything at all.

Shelter

you were my last hope for love
my shelter in the storm
my anchor on the shore
I hung onto you for so long
until you pushed me down
in despair, made me drown
now I have no hope of living
no faith in love
I have no desire left
except to be done.

My Ego Hurts

my ego hurts
and it hurts my soul
when I remember what you did
when I remember you
who am I?
my name, my face, my traits
my likes and dislikes
my identity is my ego
I serve it with much ado
but it often collapses
into the abyss of nothingness
with it, I am its slave
without it, I am nothing
tell me what to do?
my ego hurts too
when I am depressed
when I remember what you did
when I remember you.

Baggage

in New York, in Paris, in Melbourne
in London, in Berlin, in Rome
wherever in the world I travel
wherever I go and roam
I carry the baggage of memories
I always take you along

travel makes you forget the past
my travels bring your memories back.

Eyes Wide Shut

I feel light entering my heart
I feel light as a feather
I feel I am weightless
all around I see grace
I am entering into bliss
I've always waited for this
I think the time has come
my eyes are wide shut
adios to the world.

Thunderstorms

thunderstorms, heavy rains
windows are cracking by the wind
what a sad state of affairs
I only get attracted to sad art
I get anxious when I think of the future
I get depressed when I think of the past
and the thunderstorm continues
I listen to sad songs alone
cozying up in my bed
sore throat, cold and feverish sweat
is this what you expect
from a young man's life?
when will end the thunderstorm?
I am scared to go outside.

Empty

empty gaze, empty face
empty people in their empty lives
finally wounding up in graves
piling up like garbage piles
I smell sin everywhere I go
I vomit and I throw
myself at the wind
and I too sin
then I hate myself
how empty humanity has become
even the devil is surprised
where is a ray of hope?
empty streets, empty buildings, empty floors
empty mountains, empty beaches, empty stores
I only see humans, wherever I go
no ray of hope, no ray of hope.

Bygone

am I sober?
is the world drunk?
am I drunk?
is the world sober?
am I insane or is the world?
why don't I fit in?

everyplace I go
I feel a void
of happiness, I am devoid
the love I lost
would something make up for it?
sex drugs or heavenly bliss?
you were my world, my everything
without you, I am all alone
a stranger in a huge world
a voice forgotten and bygone.

Drowned in Misery

I want to go
where my heart belongs
within your embrace
singing love songs

I want to leave
this cold place
and go where the sweet breeze
kisses our feet

you remind me of our love
and I weep and cry
but not too loud and unheard
to the best I can try

I don't want people to know
that I am broken to my core
that I have drowned in misery
and you're my only shore.

Desert

do you know how an empty desert feels?
silent, vast, abandoned, and lonely

I am an empty desert that holds
silence in its heart
I am a cry gone unheard
I am an end without a start

when you reach me, you'll know
there's nowhere else to go
only silence and loneliness
and abandonment so vast.

Mysterious Girl

she is out of breath
under the sea
of tears and grief

and the emotional bloodshed
she goes through reveals
the way she feels

the way she looks
at the things she sees
is a mystery to me

she's strong yet cries
eyes wet yet smiles
she goes through a lot
and she always resides
in my thoughts that can't confine
who she is

she's a mystery to me
I see myself in her
she doesn't see that in me
tough in different ways
but we're both lonely.

Love Deprived

poverty takes the thrill out of life
but poverty is not of a single type
it's about not having things we need to survive
it's about the state of being deprived

love is a necessity
my source to survive
I am poor in love
I am love deprived.

Winter is Coming

whenever the winter comes
my heart gets sunk
deep into memories
the dim sunlight
the cold winter nights
first, bring sweet melancholy
then intense misery

my heart feels like sinking again
I feel winter is coming again.

Disappearance

how could you do this?
how could anyone do this?
how could someone be so cruel?
there's no justice
there's no mercy
you disappeared without a clue
I am filled with rage
and hate
I wish I could hurt you
but then I see you
and my heart melts
and I am all ready
to forgive you
but you don't apologize
you don't even talk
because you're not here
and then all of a sudden
I realize
it's been years
since you disappeared.

It's a Small World

someone is playing piano
in some faraway land
someone else is dancing
somewhere else
there's still daytime
in some parts of the world
and somewhere someone's crying
at the turn of the night
and here I am
looking at the moon
and thinking about you
where you would be,
what you would be doing?
would you be in someone else's arms
or would be all alone and crying

the world is a big place
yet so small.

Darkness

darkness
no light sparkles
no sign of life
silence
I think I left the tap open
there's water everywhere
my heart is overflowing
my breath is drowning
my lungs are on fire
and there's darkness
is that a shadow over there?
is that a person?
or is there no one?
I think someone's knocking
should I go and open the door?
what if there's more?
would I be able to take it?
what if there's less?
would I be disappointed?
I think there needs to be a light
I feel suffocated.

Coffin

"his coffin's too heavy,"
the townsfolk muttered in pain
"let's call more men
to give us a hand"

"but how can his coffin be so burdened
and so heavy? He was a man with no heart
at a young age, he gave it away
to some maiden who tore it apart"

"I don't care for that," said the other
"I need help to carry this burden
otherwise, I will drop it here
and I am sure no one will care
so ask for more help and bring more men
his coffin is heavy and we need more hands"

hence came more men together
tried to lift my coffin at once
all of them lifted in immense pain
shouted "his coffin is too heavy"
and put it back on the ground again

"let's open it up and see
what could possibly be

inside, there might be more than one corpse,
from the weight, it feels like"

so they tore up my coffin to have a glance
some cried with tears, some shouted in trance
to no one's surprise
only one corpse inside

and the rest of the coffin was filled with memories

Silent Since...

silence talks to me
silence talks to me in silence
after midnight, when the world is asleep
and I am drowned in your memories
I can hear myself breathing
I can hear my tears falling
silence asks me about you
and I have nothing to tell
my tears keep on falling
everything seems so quiet
at peace, so beautiful, so content
my tears fall as they fell
when you left
from that moment, since then
silence is my friend.

Sadness and Depression

sadness is something
present since centuries,
it can be found in ancient texts
since the beginning of time
depression is a recent form of misery
a modern phenomenon,
or maybe a recent discovery.

depression is when you can't have
the things you want
and sadness is when you lose
the things you had.
at least that's what I like to think
the difference is
even though I am no expert
on this topic.

I like to think that
I am not depressed but sad
because in sadness there is still
a small ray of hope
that I was good enough to have
what I once had.

Maybe Sad And Not Depressed

some grave calls me at night
some ghosts gnaw at my existence
demons have command over my soul
I feel dead withal
all the excitement has gone astray
to love's hunt, I became prey
now ghosts of past dance all night
and scare me with anxious sights
I am sad but not depressed
I hope I am being honest.

Expectations

I heard stories of lovers
growing up
my eyes would light up
with excitement in my body
and warmth in my soul
I wanted to be a lover growing up
and wanted to turn my life's tale
into a famous folklore
about love

I imagined a beloved in my fanciful thoughts
whose touch would make the days shine
whose face would be the moon
on my solitary nights

so naive and lost, was I
a dreamer living a fairy tale
I didn't know love's path would be so lonely
that I'd ruin myself in the process
and ruin my life forever

I didn't know it would hurt so much
I didn't know I would cry so much
that my eyes would run dry every night
and I would sleep with paining sighs

I didn't know love was a curse
I didn't know I prayed for my destruction.
and now I am all alone in the entire world
and now I have no one.

Years Have Passed Like This

I have spent all these
years and months
waiting for you
to return

a naive fool was I
I stopped working on myself
and let the years go by

in hope you will come back
and bring light to my life
the darkness will disappear
as soon as your moonlit face will appear

honey, it was not your fault
you are not to blame
I am to blame
starting today,
I am making a change

Sad But Not Depressed

my shirt is wet with tears
solitary nights in fear
that you will not return again
I need to cope with this pain
so let me be sad and not depressed
and think not what I have lost
but think of what I once had
it's all in our perspective that makes us depressed
it's all in our perspective that makes us sad.

More books by Ali Ashraf:

The Divine Tavern
The Rosary of Love
JAZB: Urdu Poetry with English Translation
Invocations: Islamic Sufi Poetry Collection

Your reviews are highly appreciated.